Legends of Nottinghamshire

80p

Legends of Nottinghamshire

by

Pat Mayfield

Illustrated by Steve Edgell

DALESMAN BOOKS
1976

The Dalesman Publishing Company Ltd.,
Clapham (via Lancaster), North Yorkshire.

First published 1976

ISBN: 0 85206 352 0

Printed in Great Britain by
Galava Printing Company Limited, Hallam Road, Nelson, Lancs.

Contents

The cover painting of Robin Hood is by Bruce Danz.

Introduction

VERY little appears to be known generally about the legends and lore of Nottinghamshire, and on looking at a map of folk lore we are only distinguishable by a large and rather noticeable gap. Nottingham has appeared until now as a city of industry, but with little culture of its own. This fortunately is not true, but the finding of our old customs has proved fairly difficult, for very few people ever considered writing them down and there are little bits to be found all over the place.

I am greatly indebted to Mr. L. R. Herrett of Mansfield Library, who has given so much of his spare time to finding so much of the folk lore there; also to Mr. Radcliffe of Newark Library. Mr. E. W. Mellors of Mansfield has also been of assistance to me with his details of Plough Monday and wassailing, as well as the play for Christmas called "the old 'oss".

It has been difficult to classify this information into chapters because it has rather been like putting together a jigsaw. I hope however you will find something to interest you within these pages.

The legend telling how Nottingham Goose Fair obtained its name.

1. Nottinghamshire Legends

PROBABLY the most famous item in the folk lore of Nottinghamshire, which is still as popular today as it was in years gone by, is the Goose Fair. Although the whole aspect of the fair has changed from buying in stock for the winter to an amusement for the general public, it has continued from 1290 until the present day without a break. Many of the changes have taken place gradually and were almost unnoticed by the general public; others caused quite a stir, such as the changing of the site to that on the Forest ground early in this century. Now brandy snap, toffee apples and candy floss are the seasonal fare to be found on the site, whereas in the early days the geese and livestock—which were sold to help the townsfolk stock up with provisions for the winter months—were by far the most important aspect of Goose Fair. Gradually there came minstrels and jugglers, as well as many who lived off their wits, until the well-known Nottingham Goose Fair became one of the most popular fairs in the country, as well as one of the largest.

It has been the custom for many years for the Lord Mayor to open the fair, but for some reason the ringing of the bell has become associated with the opening. This really is totally untrue. The bell was rung as a warning to all good and decent citizens that there were thieves about, and they should take care of their money. In the beginning the fair actually lasted for twenty-one days, and there is a wonderful little legendary story associated with those very early years which shows how scattered the people were at that time, and how few of them associated with anyone other than those in their own villages or farmsteads.

A farmer, who was known to have lost his wife for some reason, and was known for his hatred of all women following her loss, had brought up his three sons in total seclusion from the outside world. When the last of them came of age, he decided it was time that he should take them to Goose Fair to see how business was transacted. Before he left home with them, the farmer promised to buy each of his sons what they liked best. As they gazed about them, they asked the names of everything they saw. They came across some women all dressed in white, and demanded of their father what they were. The farmer was somewhat alarmed at the eagerness of their questioning and replied, "Those silly things are geese." Together they instantly replied, "Father, buy me a goose."

There are various tales told as to how Goose Fair came by its name, and one of the very oldest is this. A fisherman was spending a little of his free time angling in the Trent, close to Nottingham. After a while he felt a bite on the end of his line and, unlike modern anglers, he drew his line in high up in the air with the fish on the end. The fish it seems was a large pike. At the very moment that he did this a wild goose happened to be passing overhead, and on seeing the fish in the air made a grab at it and caught it. The poor goose did not realise that attached to the pike was a hook, line, rod and of course an angler, so he carried them all. The story goes on to relate how, as the goose flew over the Market Place in Nottingham, it became so exhausted with the weight that it dropped the whole lot. Strange to tell our famous angler arrived in the Square without a scratch upon his person, and to celebrate his great good fortune a holiday was declared for all the people of Nottingham, who of course greatly rejoiced on the occasion.

Goose eating at Michaelmas was considered to be very lucky, and it was supposed that

> *Who eats Goose on Michaelmas Day,*
> *Shan't money lack his debts to pay.*

It was also the custom for landlords to receive presents from their tenants of a goose.

* * *

The other custom which is almost always associated with Nottingham is the legend of Robin Hood. Now, to be fair, I have found records myself of a sheriff and others being robbed by outlaws in Nottingham Forest, or at least the part of Sherwood Forest that was in Nottinghamshire, but I have not myself found any record of who actually did the robbing. Others who have studied Robin Hood claim that they have, but Sherwood Forest extended right up into Yorkshire and down to Herefordshire, as well as into Lincolnshire. This amounts to an enormous amount of territory which lays claim to this, the most popular legendary figure of the past. Not for me I feel would it be right to either prove or disprove his living; there are so many books and ballads about him that I leave the matter entirely in my readers' hands.

*   *   *

Plough Monday was another great festive occasion in Nottinghamshire for many centuries; in fact the origins of this custom go back to the early middle ages. Originally they must have started the same, but over the centuries there were variations made according to where the plays were performed. In all probability this was because during the time of the Puritan reigns, all plays had to be mimed. No word or song was allowed in any performance at all. Now it is reasonably easy to learn the lines of a play, and to remember them when revised the following year, but to remember a mime is not nearly so easy. In consequence there was quite a variation to be found in various parts of the county. One of the severest critics of the changes which had taken place was Washington Irving who, while staying at Newstead Abbey, was invited to watch their edition of Plough Bullocking. He commented that the edition which he saw was only a very poor imitation of the mumming which had taken place for centuries.

The version which he was privileged to see went like this. All the local players were invited into the Abbey, and were requested to perform in the servants' hall. Some did antics and juggled while others prepared for the play. The play began:

> *In comes bold Anthony*
> *As bold as a mantle tree,*
> *I am come to show you sport, activity.*
> *A room, a room, a gallant room!*
> *And give us leave to sport,*
> *For in this house I do resort,*
> *It is a merry day.*
> *Step in the King of England and boldly clear the way.*

> (enter the King)

> *I am the King of England,*
> *And so boldly do appear;*
> *I've come to seek my only son,*
> *My only son and heir.*
> *If you don't agree to what I say*
> *Step in Prince George, thou valiant Knight*
> *And boldly clear the way.*

11

(enter the Prince)

I am Prince George the valiant Knight,
In fighting I took great delight,
I fought two fiery Dragons, and brought about great
*   slaughter,*
And by these means I gained Selina, the King of
*   England's Daughter.*

(at this juncture there is a skirmish and the war-
like Prince is overcome)

(enter Selina)

Who calls for Selina?

The King: *Selina I call to thee behold;*
They have killed my Prince
Oh terrible! What hast thou done?
Thou hast ruined me, and killed my son.
Is there ne'er a Doctor to be found,
To cure this deep and deadly wound?

(enter the Doctor)

Oh, yes, there is a Doctor to be found
To cure this deep and deadly wound.

The King: *What is your pay?*

Doctor: *Ten pounds is my pay.*
But as thou art an old friend, I'll take nine of thee.

The King: *What can'st thou cure?*

Doctor: *I can cure the palsy and the Gout,*
Pains within and pains without,
Bring to me a woman,
Aged three score years and ten,
I'll take her collar bone out,
And put it in again.

The King: *Then cure my son.*
Doctor: *I'll cure your son as safe and sound,*
As any man on England's Ground

(He then applies something to the lips of the youth)

Here, George, take a little of my Nip-nap,
Put it down thy licktap,
Arise, and fight again.

(accordingly George rises)

After the play had ended there were ballads recited; mostly they were those of St. George and the Dragon, and there was Morris and sword dancing to follow.

All the Plough Monday plays took place on the second Monday in January, and were probably related to the very ancient fertility rites. One particular part of the ceremonies shows this quite clearly. The money that was collected by the players was to pay for the plough lights. These were candles which were left burning in front of the shrines of the saints in all the local churches.

Mr. E. W. Mellors of Mansfield, who has sent me a copy of the play that was performed there, points out that the characters differed greatly in this part of the county. This version included the devil himself, or Beelzebub, as well as a courtier, Mickey Bent, Molly Mop, Tommy Tupp and Slasher.

Perhaps the biggest variation of all was to be found in Shelford, for here the festivities lasted the whole day long. Early in the morning, the children of the village covered their faces with red ochre and, after decking their hats with coloured ribbons and streamers, would tour the village collecting all types of cakes and sweets. These were distributed among all the children in Shelford. The question that each child had to ask before anything could be given to him was, "Please do you remember the Plough Bullock?" In the evening the young men would blacken their faces before setting out on their round. They had a tin with them to collect coins. Lastly came the men who pulled the plough behind them. The plough had been especially cleaned and decorated for the occasion; it had ribbons and bows, and as the men journeyed along they sang:

They were treated with ale and food at the houses they visited, but woe betide anyone who gave nothing, for the ground around the doors of their house would be ploughed up, and with the snow, frosts and wet, there was little chance of repairing the damage before the summer.

After the Reformation of the Church, much of the custom changed. Before that date the village priest played a part in the plays, and the plough lights burned in order that blessing would be given to the crops of the coming year. Once the Reformation had taken place, and the long period had passed when all fun and frolics were forbidden, the plays started to be held in the local public houses and inns. Another peculiar characteristic about these celebrations was that at no time was a woman allowed to take part. All the women's parts were played by smooth-faced boys, even to the part of Maid Marian, for both she and Robin Hood appeared in some versions of the play.

Although the older people of the county had let the play die by 1850, the young men of Mansfield were still performing their version at the turn of this century. The date was, however, altered and the play was performed more often than not during the Christmas holidays. Instead of ploughing at that time they would perform practical jokes like tying doors together, or upsetting water butts. The householders, too, had become less superstitious, and would often be ready for the visitors, chasing them off with a red hot poker.

Looking through the very old records, I find a piece written by Mr. A. S. Buxton, which says: "About the year 1675 a traveller named Thomas Baskerville came to Mansfield and wrote, 'Mansfield, a Town made famous amongst country people by means of that ballad or song called the "Gelding of the Devil" has one fair church in it, and little more can be said of it'. The music to this ballad is published in number 7 of Cecil Sharp's Country Dance Tunes, and the figure of the dance itself in part 4 of his Country Dance Book. Cecil Sharp does not know the words of the Ballad, and was unaware of its Mansfield origin, until this Baskerville Letter was pointed out to him, but says that undoubtedly the dance was founded on this Ballad. As you will find, the music is lively and the dance pretty and simple being a round for six of a now progressive order, belonging to the class of those from which our modern quadrilles and Lancers were originated." This was a ballad performed as part of the Plough Monday celebrations, as also was the dance.

*　　*　　*

The whole county was also involved in the celebration of Mothering Sunday, as indeed was the rest of the country. It does, however, have a particular significance for Nottinghamshire, as it was a woman from Coddington, a Miss Constance Painswick Smith, who revived the custom in the early years of this century. Historians were then openly boasting that Mothering Sunday was one custom that they had managed to do without. However, Miss Smith not only wrote a book about the day, which she felt was a celebration well worth keeping, but worked so hard for its

14

revival that an altar was placed by Bishop Barry in Coddington church in 1951, which was to her memory.

Mothering Sunday has altered vastly from its original custom, for in the days before it was forgotten it was the one day of the year which was given as a holiday to young people who were placed in service in order that they might visit their parents. The presents taken were made by them all through the year, and one was taken for each parent. The children were placed in service at a very young age, and if they had not have been many would not have survived. At least in the houses where they were placed they had a bed and food and clothing, even if they were treated cruelly if you judge by today's standards. If many of them had stayed at home, they would have died of starvation, especially in the times when there was little work. Many of the antique samplers that are now so much prized by antique dealers were the work of those youngsters who were taught to sew by their mistresses.

In fact the custom of Mothering Sunday goes right back to the early beginnings of the Church, for it is supposed to be the day on which the mother of all the goddesses, Hilaria by name, was converted to the Mother Church. The date for that was supposed to have been March the eighth. It is a pity that the revival has become just a time for extra trade for the florists and card manufacturers, instead of a gift made especially to thank mother for all she does.

In the olden days, when the children arrived home on Mothering Sunday, they would in Nottinghamshire find a special dish of food prepared for them; this was called fermity. To make this dish whole grains of corn were boiled until they were soft and plump, and then the water was drained off. The grains were then placed into milk which had been heated together with spices. It was only ever served on this one day of the year.

*   *   *

Twelfth night was also a time for celebration in the county and one where all the family got together. On this day a special rich fruit cake was baked, and into the dough were placed a silver coin, a ring and a thimble. Whoever received the coin in their slice of the cake would not be without money for the year, whoever got the ring would be the next to get married, and the thimble symbolised the fact that they would never marry.

First footing took place here, too, but not with coal as we do now. In fact a gold coin was placed outside the door by the head of the household for the first footer to bring in with him. This was to ensure the family having sufficient wealth for the rest of the year. To find that we now use coal, as do all those who first foot everywhere else in the country, seems strange, for in fact Nottinghamshire was the first to mine coal, and the first wheels ever to run on rails were from Strelley pit to Wollaton. This was long before the days of railways; the wagons were pushed by men, and later pulled by pit ponies.

Another New Year custom which was carried out all over the county was that of wassailing. The young women of the local village or town went from door to door on New Year's Eve, specially dressed up for the occasion. They would each carry a bowl filled with a brew of ale, toast and roasted apples. These were well seasoned with nutmeg, sugar and many other spices. The bowl itself would be gaily decorated with ribands and evergreens, and was offered to the householder after they had sung. The women who took part in this custom were generally the poorer ones in the community, and that is why there were no objections to the collection of money after the singing. One of the verses of the song went something like this:

> *Good Master at your door, our Wassail we begin,*
> *We are all maidens poor, so we pray you let us in,*
> *And drink our Wassail, All Hail wassail,*
> *Wassail, Wassail and drink our wassail.*

*   *   *

Years ago, when the Duke of Newcastle replaced the old Castle with his Town House, the races were held each year on the Forest. The Duke usually came here for the races, and on one evening during his stay he would open the house to the people of Nottingham, when they could eat and drink as much as they pleased at the Duke's expense. On one of these occasions, the Chief Gingerbread Maker of the town (and that is exactly how he is described in the history books, including the capital letters) came out of the Castle, and unfortunately turned the wrong way. After falling down the full length of the Castle Rock, he picked himself up and, apart from a few bruises and scratches, made his way home unhurt. This man must have held quite an important position in the town for his exploit to be described in such a fashion, and yet as far as one can see there is no gingerbread specially made in Nottingham now.

Another incident at the Duke's house which caused much amusement in later years was that concerning the Duke's favourite statue. It was a marble horse set upon a lintel above the main door of the Castle. To all visitors the Duke would proudly show off this statue, and felt justly proud of the workmanship which had gone into it. After the place was burned down, during the Parliamentary Reform riots in 1831, the statue—which had fallen from its lintel—was found to have had three marble legs, but the fourth was a wooden one. Presumably some clever carpenter had replaced the one which must have been broken when it was put into place.

*　　*　　*

When the punishment for minor offences was no longer allowed in the markets of Nottingham, the people in the villages decided that the perpetrators of these minor offences would not go unchallenged and unpunished. It was in this way that the custom called "Riding the Stang" came into being. It was felt very strongly at the time that the best form of punishment for these minor offences, as far as the law was concerned, was public ridicule. The time that this form of custom became established was after the abolition of the pillory, the ducking stool, and the stocks, and the country folk were much more incensed about the change than were the townsfolk.

If a husband was known to beat his wife or allow himself to be "henpecked" it would not be long before he found himself being serenaded by the people of the village. The musical instruments which were used by the serenaders were such as frying and warming pans, tea kettles on which they drummed with a key, the lids of iron pots which served as cymbals, fire pokers and tongs. Marrow bones were also added to the noise which serenaded the person concerned. The villagers would assemble outside the offenders house and salute him with an outburst of their "music". Some villages went even further and made an effigy of the person which was placed in a cart and carted around the village, until they came to the home of the person concerned. Then all the villagers would sing out verses, such as:

> *With a ran tan tan,*
> *This man has been lickin' his good woman*
> *For what, and for why?*
> *For eating so much when hungry,*
> *And drinking so much when dry,*
> *With a ran tan tan, etc.*

After this the effigy of the man would be burned and other verses sung which listed his crimes and promised that he would go to hell if he continued in this type of behaviour. This was still a very popular form of rough justice a hundred years ago, and no intervention was ever made by the law as far as I can trace.

*　　*　　*

The May Day celebrations were also among the very ancient fertility rites. Although May Day—or Labour Day as it has become known—has not been forgotten, the whole meaning and the customs associated with it have completely changed. If you wish to look at the customs as they were, you have to go back a couple of centuries to find the original rites still being carried out. As soon as the sun rose on May Day morning, all the youngsters would rise from their beds and go out into the forests to collect flowers and foliage. They would return at about break-fast time noisy and hungry, playing any musical instrument that they could lay their hands on, including very often the leaves from trees with a comb, as we today would use a comb and paper. They would then set about decorating all the doors and windows of their own houses, and those of their neighbours and sweethearts, with garlands of flowers. Almost all the villages had a maypole and these too would be festooned with garlands of flowers and gaily coloured ribands. After they had all been home to eat, the dancing would begin. One of the most unsual, which was typically Nottinghamshire, was the Milkmaids' Dance. They would borrow as many plates as they could, and making a pyramid on top of their pails, using tankards between the plates, they would dance round the village to all their customers. After knocking on each door they would be given a small gratuity for their services throughout the year.

Gradually even the custom of having a maypole has ceased, although there are some people making attempts to revive it. There are unfortunately few forests left either, and efforts are being made by many societies to try to preserve the wild flowers which were so prolific 200 years ago. Already, many of them have become extinct.

*　　*　　*

It may seem very unusual to us today that even 150 years ago it was quite customary for people never to leave the streets where they were born. There is a story of a young woman who had been very ill, and lived in the town of Nottingham. As she had rela-

18

tions in Ruddington it was decided to take her there for a holiday, hoping that the change would do her good. She was terrified at the sight of the fields, and loudly and solemnly declared that "she would never have left home, if she had known that the world was so big." The total distance that she had travelled at the end of her journey was five miles.

Another popular day among the young people was the 29th of May, formerly known as Oak and Nettle Day. Going out in the early morning they would decorate their caps and coats with oak leaves. In order to make sure that everyone else did the same, they would arm themselves with a handful of stinging nettles. Any person that they met on the road was asked to show the oak. As long as they could show one single leaf they were safe; if they couldn't they were well stung about their hands and face. Having had this cruelty inflicted upon them, they were given an oak sprig in order that they would not be attacked again. This custom was only allowed to continue until noon, but in the north of the county they collected eggs from one year to the next, and people without their oak would be pelted with these. It was the eggs which really upset the older people and gradually the police were called in more and more to get rid of the rascals who performed such tricks. Eventually Oak and Nettle Day was banned altogether, and if anyone should dare to try such antics today they would quickly be dealt with.

2

Religious Folklore

AT one time there were two villages in Nottinghamshire which were both swallowed up by earthquakes. The first was lost about 1185, at the time of the earthquake which split Lincoln Cathedral from top to bottom. One day the village of Raleigh was there, and the next day it had completely disappeared. Raleigh stood where Radleigh Farm is now, on the road between Oxton and Southwell. The people, not understanding the nature of earthquakes, honestly believed that the village had descended to a lower level, and they believed the same when Grimstone disappeared. Now we are aware that Grimstone was there in 1434, for we have a tax return for that date. After that, nothing. Grimstone once stood where the village of Wellow now stands, on the road between Newark and Ollerton. The people of Nottinghamshire were still paying homage to these two places during the last century. Every Christmas morning they would make pilgrimages to the sites of these villages and, laying their ears to the ground, would swear that they could hear the church bells sounding out their Christmas chimes under the ground. The fear which the first earthquake caused among the people was terrific, and immediately a painting of St. Christopher appeared which covered the whole of the north wall of St. Mary's church. The reason that St. Christopher was the saint chosen was that he was thought to be the only one who had sufficient power to prevent tempests and earthquakes. The figure, although crude, remained on the side of the church for more than 300 years.

*   *   *

Shrove Tuesday was a feast greatly looked forward to by the poor people of Trowell, Wollaton and Cossall, for it was on that day that the Honourable and Lady Willoughby opened their doors at Aspley Hall for a pancake feast. They were relatives of the Willoughby family of Wollaton Hall, and they supplied lard and butter, frying pans and fire for the festival. We are told that there were never less than ten families at any one time partaking of the hospitality. On high-backed chairs, the Honourable and Lady Willoughby watched the proceedings, and joined in the general laughter and chatter of the families. It was quite customary for Lady Willoughby to remark that "another half dozen children would make you more efficient" to any young woman who missed catching her pancake when it was tossed, and of course everyone joined in the laughter. One of the few rules which governed this treat was that all pancakes had to be tossed properly.

A mysterious figure in black was to be seen in the kitchens on these occasions. He would be walking round muttering, but was ignored by everyone present as if he was not there. He is described as being very tall and pale, lifting his hands at each family he passed, and muttering. Apart from being seen very occasionally in the woods of the Hall, no-one knew who or what he was until many years later. He was around at the time when Catholicism was outlawed, and Catholics from all over Nottingham would make their way individually to Aspley Hall on feast days. It was here that Mass was said, and feasts were remembered. The man in black was in fact a priest in hiding, and was pronouncing dedication over the food being prepared. How many people knew of his existence we do not know, but he was never betrayed—even though there was a price on the head of all Catholics—probably because the Willoughby family were loved and respected by their tenants and workers.

After the families had taken their fill of pancakes, each man, woman and child would be given ale. There was a quart for each of the men, a pint for the women and a gill for each child. In those days it was customary to drink beer, instead of water, for the sewerage ran in the streets and it was very rare to find even wells which were unpolluted. All over the county it was usual for the first pancake made in each house to be fed to a cockerel. Even in the towns it was usual to find that people kept chickens in their yards, and often pigs as well. Eventually there was an outcry against this, but that did not occur until the middle of the eighteenth century when there was a large influx of people for the knitting and lace trades and as a consequence the houses were built closer together. To add to this confusion, people from outlying villages were building town houses as well as those they already had in the country. The smell must have been atrocious to say the least.

All over the county, long before hot cross buns came into being, people always used to buy an extra loaf on Good Friday. This they would keep and use throughout the year. A mouthful or two was supposed to cure all manner of ills. When hot cross buns were introduced, all the baker was allowed to do was to mark a cross onto the bun with his knife. People were also very specific about the shape of the bun. On no account was it to be triangular; it had to be perfectly round in shape.

*   *   *

A fact very little known in Nottinghamshire is that we have a shrine which was much in use even before 1100. Although it has been destroyed once in 1538, its popularity has never ceased altogether and is now increasing. This shrine is Our Lady of Egmanton, which is situated in the small village of Egmanton about 1½ miles from Tuxford on the Great North Road. In fact the church is the only one for many miles around to bear the name of "Our Lady". It is actually on the site of Ladywood and it is believed there may have been a sighting of the Virgin Mary in early times—it is thought this is how the church and parish came by their name. There are many carved crosses on the doorways of the church which are almost certainly medieval in origin; they are also to be found on the pillars on the north aisle of the church. The crosses were usually cut to endorse vows made whilst in the presence of the shrine. Pens were placed over the sacred well in 1547, and by this means it has been preserved. According to the tradition the actual shrine was on the northern wall of the sanctuary and was within the rood screen.

After the dissolution by Henry VIII, a very great deal of even this out-of-the-way shrine was wrecked in order to bring the country to conformity to the king's will. It was purely from memory of the old people that the shrine was restored with the church in 1897. The present shrine was designed by Sir Ninian Comper and decorated in the Gothic tradition—it is an image of Our Lady, crowned with the Holy Child. The first organised pilgrimage of modern times took place in 1929 from Leicester, and since then the numbers and distance of the pilgrimages have vastly increased. The restoration of this type of work always takes a great deal of time, and the work is still going on, as and when the money for it becomes available.

Another church which was noted for its beauty was that of East Bridgford. There was at one time a tradition that a boy would play the flute from the gallery of the church. Within the building and over the chancel arch was a painting in moulded plaster, not only of the royal coat-of-arms, complete with lion and unicorn, but also the Lord's Prayer in gilt and moulded in the same way.

A peculiar sort of memorial is to be found in Bunny church.

It is dedicated to the Baronet of Bunny, one Sir Thomas Parkyns, of whom I shall write more in a later chapter. His monument is on the north wall of the church, and shows him in a wrestling posture ready for one of his famous holds. On the other side is a monument of the wrestler having been cut down by time.

*   *   *

A story associated with Newark church dates back to the early Middle Ages. In those days there were no roads which led from one place to another; there were mere bridle paths which one man and his horse might pass along. Newark, being on the banks of the Trent, was surrounded by quite dangerous marshes. The events with which we are concerned occurred in November when the fog was thick upon the ground. A Mr. Gopher was travelling towards Newark from the north when he realised that he was well and truly lost among the marshes with no chance of finding his way. It was customary in those days for the church bells to be rung one hour before the evening service on Sunday, so Mr. Gopher was able by following the sound to find his way to Newark. The whole story is actually legendary, for there are no records of the money Mr. Gopher reputedly left to ensure that the bells would always be rung at dusk. This custom is now extinct, but the tradition itself continues and an annual Gopher Dinner is held for the bell-ringers every November.

A custom which had died out, but was revived in 1974 on the request of the late Mayoress, Mrs. York, was the giving of loaves to the people of Newark. Originally this custom resulted from a "miracle" during the Civil War. It was started more than 330 years ago, when Newark was under siege by the Parliamentarian troops. In Newark Market Place there lived a man by the name of Hercules Clay, with his family. One night he dreamed three times that his house was on fire. After the third dream, Mr. Clay could no longer contain himself, so he made his family get up and dress and personally hurried them all out into the street. To all the family it appeared to be a mad whim of their father; after all, turning out of one's house at three o'clock in the morning was not a normal thing to do. They had not been outside ten minutes when a "bomb" fell directly onto their house, setting it on fire. On the other side of the street lived the Governor of Newark, and it was at his house that the "bomb" was aimed.

In order that the whole town might be aware of his deliverance from destruction, Hercules Clay made an endowment on the parish church of £200. Some of the money was to be used to

have a sermon preached in the church on the nearest Sunday to
March 11th, when the incident happened, and the interest was
to be spent to give the poor of the parish a penny loaf on that
date. In the beginning this was distributed by the church, but
some jiggery-pokery took place. After receiving their loaf, some
people took it home and came back and rejoined the queue.
Eventually the church became so worried about the situation
that it asked the Town Hall to take over the distribution. This
it did, but to ensure fairness all the recipients were locked into
a room until all the bread had been distributed. The practice
of distribution was discontinued about 1860, and the money used
for various works for the poor of Newark. In 1933 it was used
for the unemployed; on other occasions it was given to welfare
centres and workhouses. The service held in the parish to
enlighten everyone on the wonderful deliverance of Hercules
Clay and his family has however continued, although now the
sermon is preached at the tradesmen's service each year. The
revival of the custom has solved the problem of who should
receive the bread by giving it only to the regular choirboys of
the church.

*　　　*　　　*

Dunblain Chapel was erected behind Flawforth church in Ruddington. There is no written record as to the reason for its
building, but the oral legend goes something like this:— A
cheerful man who was appointed as swineherd was set to work
looking after his pigs at the back of Flawforth church. A gentleman who came by was so entranced by the boy's cheerful outlook
on life that, after enquiring about his parents and family, he
persuaded the boy to go away with him. When the gentleman
died, the swineherd came into possession of all his property.
Many years afterwards he returned to his native village only to
find that both his parents were dead and their graves were near
the church. He paid for a tomb to be erected over their graves
and on it had their figures cut and a dog placed at their feet.
These graves were eventually walled in, and the place became
known as Dunblain Chapel after the name of the swineherd's
parents.

*　　　*　　　*

The legend of Hercules Clay, who as the result of a dream saved himself
and his family from being burnt to death.

Many years ago the people of Shelford became much talked about for they set a fashion which was as peculiar as it was gaudy. Red lapels and red waistcoats could be seen worn by the men from all over the village. The material from which they were made was velvet. This continued for some time before the local clergyman, who was reported to be both sagacious and pious, discovered that the origin of the fashion was as peculiar as it was to him lamentable. The village tailor by sheer chance happened to be the church sexton and the whole story began here. Shelford is the burial place of the Earls of Chesterfield and the sexton had "borrowed" the red velvet from the coffins of the sleepers for the villagers' decoration. The vicar wrote to the Earl in the greatest humility, lamenting most bitterly the misdemeanour of his sexton and of the unhallowed desecration which had taken place. In reply, his lordship asked him to moderate his excess of sorrow, and to join him in the admiration and commending of providential ingenuity of the sexton-tailor (his lordship was well known for his wit), and for bringing into use that which his ancestors had consigned to decay into the dust!

*   *   *

A legend attached to Gotham church was the sermon given by the minister one Ash Wednesday. It was customary for him to have a collection on that day. On this particular day he stated as usual that the time of the year had come for fasting, prayer and the giving of alms. They must also come to confession and absolution. He then went on to tell them that he did not think that two men in the whole of the parish knew their Paternoster. As for fasting, he claimed that they had not had one good meal of meat in the year and, he asked, what alms can you give when you already have nothing? So he urged them to abstain from all drink during Lent, but one fellow rose up against the minister: "Is there not an old proverb that says that fish should swim?"

"Yes," replied the minister, "but they must swim in water."

"I crave your mercy," replied the fellow, "I thought that a fish should have swum in fine ale, for I have been told that." (At this time with the sewerage running in the streets and polluting all the rivers and brooks, it was safer to drink ale than water.)

The seven men of Gotham then came to confession, and the priest was hard put to find a penance that he could give them. He told the first that as he could not say his Paternoster he should work diligently all the week, and accumulate the money for a feast on Sunday. To make sure that he did this he told the

man he would join him. In this way he went through his parish-
ioners making sure that each feasted with the minister on a
different day. In this way, said the minister, "you who are beggars
yourselves will indeed spend your alms upon yourselves."

*   *   *

A legend which goes right back before the origin of Christian-
ity is that whereby a boy child was presented at the tabernacle
on the fortieth day after birth. The custom really was that the
eldest boy in each family should be presented to God as a
future priest. He was usually bought back into the family by
the present of two white doves in exchange; this was adopted
into some churches and was the custom now known as cradle
rocking. For some reason or other, the custom lasted for longer
in Austria than it did in England. The church at Blidworth is
one of only two churches in the whole world named St. Mary's of
the Purification. This is why the rocking ceremony was revived
here, and if you look at the stained glass windows in the church
you will find them dedicated to children in some form or other.
The Feast of the Purification is on February 2nd, and the rocking
ceremony is held on the nearest Sunday to that date.

The child who is born the closest to Christmas Day is taken
to evensong on that Sunday, and is carried in procession from
the church door. After the second lesson, the parents go to the
altar rail with the child, who is given to the vicar and is dedicated to God in the way of the Church. In front of the altar is a
cradle (the one used now is more than 150 years old), which has
been decorated by the ladies of the church with wild snowdrops
and violets until the hood is covered as if it were a bonnet. The
child usually remains in the crib until the last hymn is sung, after
which he is handed back to his mother by the vicar. If you decide
to go and have a look at Blidworth church it is worthwhile
noting that the pillars on the west side of the nave are black.
This was done for the funeral of King George II. The unfortunate
part of the matter was that, having put the paint on, the people
found the stain would not come off.

*   *   *

Aslockton is very proud of its associations with Archbishop
Cramner. You can still see the site of the old archbishop's home,
although the place where it stood has now been used for another

27

house. The local pub is of course the Cramner Arms. Some parts of the old chapel walls are, I believe, still to be seen. Whatton was the parish church of the people of Aslockton, and it is there you must look if you wish to find the graves of the Cramner family. There is a slab inserted in the centre of the north aisle which is dedicated to the father of the archbishop. It turns out that the archbishop was his second son; no-one is quite sure which school he went to, for he wrote little about his past. We do however know that he went to a grammar school and that after his father had been dead for five years his mother decided to send him to Jesus College, Cambridge. It was well known that when the Archbishop took a rest he would come to his brother's home in Aslockton. It appears from the old documents that he had some property here of his own. In 1527 Edward VI granted to the Archbishop the sum of £429 13s. from the churches of Whatton and Aslockton with the advowson (making him Patron of both churches), although they were under Welbeck Abbey.

*   *   *

Southwell Minster, now of course known as the mother church of the area, has had a claim on the people of this county for many centuries. A man by the name of Paulinus was thought to have founded the Minster and indeed some of his early work can still be seen today. He was the first missionary to reach these parts, and was reputed to have a great gift of oratory. It may seem a peculiar thing to us now to know that the waters of the river Trent were frequently used by Paulinus for baptism and other sacred rites. Gradually the church progressed from wood to stone and became a favourite haven for many of the Archbishops of York. The setting at Southwell has always been a beautiful one, and kings and bishops alike have fallen in love with the place to the extent that some have even called it a rival to York and Canterbury.

In the early part of the eighteenth century Nottinghamshire had its own Gretna Green, and it was the village of Fledborough which became renowned as such. At the time the rector of this tiny scattered village community was one by the name of Mr. Sweetapple. He, like the blacksmith on the Scottish border, fettered the couple together with a chain which could not be broken until the death of one of the partners or a divorce took place. He was not concerned for whom he performed these services, and people came from miles away to be married in this fashion.

The church of St. Peter at East Drayton is also well worth

visiting. In the belfry you will find a hundred rings all painted on the wall in red ochre. The initials of the couples married there are beside the rings. These are in fact almost a century's weddings, for the first inscription was in 1777 and the last in 1865. In the days when this was the custom, a peal of bells was sounded while the young couple signed the marriage register. A large plum loaf and a cheese was then taken to the belfry for the ringers, who shared this fare with all the children who made their way and paraded into the tower.

3

Legends and Love Trysts

THERE are several legends associated with Gotham. Quite why this should be we do not know, but the first originated way back in history at the time when King John was on the throne, having arranged for his brother King Richard to be kidnapped in Austria while on his way to the Crusades. Although this particular legend was not written down for many years, we can be certain that there is more than a grain of truth in it. In those ancient and far off days, it was believed that wherever the king walked was from that day on a royal highway with general access for all who so required it. The countryside was wild at the time, and it was necessary for scouts always to proceed a day in front of the king so that if the road was not safe he could be warned in time and continue on his journey another way. Other travellers too were on the road or bridle paths, which was really all they were, and the coming of the king was almost always news to the villagers long before the scouts of the king's party arrived. So it was in Gotham.

Now in order for King John to get to Nottingham Castle, and pass through Gotham, it meant that he would inevitably have to walk across their best meadow. In a small community, grazing land could mean the difference between the life and death of the village, especially as so much of Gotham was gypsum outcrop. To put up an opposition of arms would have been ridiculous, for the villagers would have been hopelessly outnumbered, and would have added to the king's displeasure. It was therefore necessary for other means to be found to dissuade the king from passing through. One thing that all men of that era were afraid of was lunacy. There were no doctors to cure it, and as far as possible those who were considered harmless were left alone—others were tried as witches.

The people of Gotham therefore devised the cleverest trick possible to keep the king away; they played the harmless fools. When the advance party arrived, they found some of the men trying to rake the reflection of the moon out of the pond, swearing that it was a cheese. They were armed with hay rakes for the job, and you may guess at the bickering which was going on. Others were placing a fence around a wood where a cuckoo had roosted for the night. They explained that if they could keep the cuckoo, it would always be spring in Gotham. Others were rolling cheeses down the hill towards Nottingham (this is still known as Cheese Hill, although the road has had to be altered to make it safer). They told the advance party that they were sending the cheeses to Nottingham Market; after all it was downhill all the way, and doing it this way saved them a journey. The king as well as his party considered that the men of Gotham were fools to be avoided at all costs. The village meadow was saved, as well as the people. Can you wonder that it was not long before they became known as the Wise Fools of Gotham?

There is another legend of Gotham—one about the housewives who sat in the alehouse discussing among themselves the advantages of their husband's choice of themselves as wives. The first claimed that she never did anything and therefore was very reliable for being the same every day. In fact she kept so much to this routine that she never even went to church on a Sunday, but said her prayers in the alehouse where she was always to be found. She felt that the regularity of her behaviour, and the prayers she said, sped her husband on his way and did him more good than all she could do for him in a housewifely fashion. The second wife said that she was good to her husband by the saving of candles in winter, for both she and all her family went to bed by daylight all the year round. The third wife claimed to save much of her keep by drinking only ale, eating very little bread or meat as she did not care much for either, but she did admit that she drank a gallon of ale a day. The fourth wife said that she neither ate nor drank at home, but walked to Nottingham where she sat in a tavern and ate and drank whatever was given to her. This saved her husband all of her keep. The fifth wife said that she never gave her company more to one man than another; in this way she never became a bore. The sixth wife said that provided she spent all her time in other people's homes her husband always had flax and wood to spare. She was using none of it by working for other people, and thus she saved him greatly. The seventh wife said that she saved money for her husband by sitting all day at other people's fires, and the eighth said that as pork, mutton and chickens were always so dear, she spent the money on pigs, rabbits and capons. The ninth wife declared that she saved much of her husband's money which she would ordinarily have spent on soap, for instead of washing once a week she washed only once a quarter. The ale housewife was the last to speak, declaring that she saved her husband more than all the rest of them for, whereas she used only to drink a drop of her husband's ale, she now drank it all and by so doing prevented any of it from going sour.

* * *

Another legend, but this time of Nottingham, dates back many years, and there is no real evidence as to where it took place. As a young and very handsome gypsy walked down the road towards the entrance to Nottingham, he saw some large notices and stopped to read them. The notices told of a great lady of the city who was in want of a husband. When he arrived in the town he made enquiries about this lady, only to find that she was very rich and beautiful and probably a princess. The description of the man she wanted could he felt quite easily be himself. After thinking things over for a while, he decided to present himself for the job the following morning. In the meantime, however, some Nottingham workmen warned him that the lady had already had seven husbands and, what was more, no-one knew what had become of them. This put him on his guard but such was his need for money and a roof over his head that he decided to go anyway.

The following morning the young man presented himself at the gate of the lady's house. The door was answered by a maid who asked if he had come to marry her mistress. When he replied that he had, the girl took him upstairs and the lady immediately decided that he was the man she wanted to marry. A grand wedding was arranged and all went very well, except that when the young man awoke during the night the lady was not there. In the morning, however, there she was, back in bed beside him and asking him if he had slept well. Although he was worried he said nothing, and waited until the following night, only to find that the same thing happened. On the third night the man only pretended to go to sleep. When his wife slipped out of bed as she had done before, she dressed herself quietly and went out of the bedroom. Her husband slipped on a gown and followed her at a safe distance, and was surprised to find that she took a small pathway which had at the end of it some graves. Some of them had obviously been disturbed, and the woman got down on her hands and knees and scooped away the earth. Her husband then crept up on her, and asked what she was doing. He saw her eating and demanded what it was: "Corpse you wretch, corpse", came her reply.

A much more recent Nottingham legend is about the statue of Queen Victoria, which stood in the centre of Nottingham Square, and that of Sir Samuel Morley, which was at one time outside the Theatre Royal. The legend said that every Christmas Eve, at the stroke of midnight, Sir Samuel would step down from his statue and walk down the Market Street. After arriving in the Square he would bow to Queen Victoria and then return the way he had come. The statue of Sir Samuel was deemed to be in a dangerous position when the motor car really started to take over the streets, so the City Council in its wisdom decided that it should be removed and set up at the entrance to the Eastcroft Depot. This is where the story really begins. The council workmen came and very carefully placed the statue onto the back of a lorry where they tied it securely. As the lorry passed along Wheeler Gate, Sir Samuel caught sight of a dressmaker's dummy completely naked in a shop window. He was so astounded at what he saw that he leapt from the lorry and broke into thousands of pieces on the road. Sir Samuel is still remembered, however, for a bust of him stands in the Arboretum.

*　　*　　*

A much older legend is that of a Nottinghamshire clergyman who went to London, and decided one evening to attend a performance at the Drury Lane Theatre. At the entrance there was a large crowd awaiting admission, and while the pressure of the crowd was great he felt someone go into his pocket in order to steal his watch. He managed to reach his fob pocket and found it empty. Seeing a suspicious man close by, he whispered to him and charged him with stealing his watch. The next moment he felt a watch being pushed into his hand, and heard whispered instructions to say nothing about it. Quite naturally the clergyman put away the watch, but this time made sure that it was in a safer place than his fob pocket. With the entertainment of the evening, he thought no more of the incident until he reached the inn where he was staying. On going to his bedroom the first thing he saw was the black ribbon and the pendants of his watch. Examining the watch he had received in the crowd, it was a truly magnificent affair valued at somewhere between forty and fifty pounds. He realised that it must have been stolen from someone only a short time before he had been given it by the thief. Although the clergyman advertised it in all the newspapers, no-one ever came forward to claim it. For the rest of his life he enjoyed telling the tale of the way he had outwitted a quick-witted thief.

*　　*　　*

33

A man who lived to be a legend, and was celebrated as such in his own lifetime, was one by the name of William Walker of East Bridgford. He was a bricklayer, and worked at his trade from the time he was 12 until he was 86. He was very proud of the fact that he had assisted with the building of the first railway station in Nottingham. He had seen Queen Victoria before her Coronation at Westminster Abbey, and was presented to King George V when he visited Nottingham in July 1928. He was the oldest man in England when he died aged 107 years and 51 days, proved by the parish registers of East Bridgford.

*   *   *

Clifton, now an integral part of Nottingham in spite of the impression it gives of being a town apart, was really made famous by the tragedy of the Fair Maid of Clifton. Most people are aware of the poem written by Henry Kirk White, whose ballad became very famous. He was a young man when he wrote it, and unfortunately he too died young. In the British Museum there are several versions of this story of young Margaret who died within the area of Clifton Grove; if you should ever wish to find them they come under the title of Bateman's tragedy. The story was even converted into a play and performed on the stage.

Sir Robert Clifton, Bart., M.P., wrote his version of the story about 150 years ago: "A perjured maid, sheltering from a storm was struck by lightning, and carried from the Grove into the Clifton Deeps below; and as many people say, curiously enough from that day to this the land down which she fell has remained arid to this day!"

Throsby, referring to the occurrence, states: "Here Tradition says, the Clifton Beauty, who was debauched and murdered by her sweetheart, was hurled down the precipice into a watery grave. The place has long been held in veneration by lovers."

There was a ballad about the same incident written by Captain Barker from the dictation of the schoolmistress of Wells Hospital. It was published in "Walks Around Nottingham" in 1835, Captain Barker using the pseudonym "A Wanderer". According to this version, Margaret was very choosey about her boy friends, although she had many would-be followers. At last a young man by the name of Bateman came along, and after a time they fell in love. In order to signify this they made an oath and cut in half a golden coin, having half each. For reasons of his work Mr. Bateman was unable to see his sweetheart for three months, and when he returned to her he arrived on the day she was marrying a rich old landowner, one Germain by name. Margaret denied her vows, and he vowed that she would never know any peace. He hung himself with a stout cord on her front door. As she was pregnant no evil could come to her until after the child was born. One night, although she was being watched, all those in the room fell asleep. Margaret crept out of the room, leaving her new born infant, and went into the grove where she committed suicide by throwing herself off the steepest bank into the river.

Kirk White uses much the same story in his poem, but states that eventually it was Bateman who first threw himself into the Trent at the thought of his beloved laying in another man's arms. Tradition says that Margaret was carried away by demons into the dell. Now which of these stories is the true one, if indeed any of them are, I will leave entirely to your discretion, but the story has been so long in traditional tales that there is almost bound to be a grain of truth in it somewhere.

*　　*　　*

Another folk lore love story is that of the Republican officer and the maid of Broxtowe. This dates back to the time when the Republican armies were in possession of this village. The officer concerned was the commander of the fort; he was a gentleman in all his ways, although he was a very firm Protestant and was uncompromising Republican in his politics. The object of his affections was Agnes Willoughby, who was of Aspley Wood Hall and of course a Catholic. The commander was Captain Thornhalgh, the son of the famous soldier who lost his life in a battle with the Scots at Prestonpans.

Captain Thornhalgh rescued Lady Agnes while she was returning from visiting the poor and sick in the village of Bilborough. Always during these times of civil commotions there were many thieves and vagabonds waiting for the unwary in woods and on bridle paths. Many were victims of the war, others were opportunists who found this an easy way of living. The Captain was strolling along with his Bible in his hand when he heard cries for help, as if a young lady were fighting for her honour or her life. Making his way to where the noise was coming from, he found that three wretches had hurled her to the ground and were running away across the fields. He took out his pistol and gently escorted the maiden to her father's house. A visit by Captain Thornhalgh to the house on the following morning to enquire after the lady also served to break down the normal barrier between the Protestant and the Papist. Gradually the two fell in love. Her parents of course had great regard for the Captain in view of his personal courage in going to the rescue of their

The story of St. Catherine's Well, Newark, and two knights—Sir Everard
Bevercotes and Sir Guy Saucimer.

daughter without heed of the consequences to himself. In view of this they could no longer regard him as a Puritan, a Round-head, and a rebel. On the other hand they could not agree to the lovers becoming married with so much difficulty between them.

It was then that fate in the form of army duty reared its ugly head. Captain Thornhalgh was sent for by Colonel Hutchinson to take as many men as could be spared from the fort of Brox-towe to help with the siege of Newark. The Captain managed to send a message to Agnes by way of a trusty soldier. Two days later he was preparing to make an assault on Shelford Manor House, which at that time had been turned into a fort. For reasons of the actual situation of the house, it was a place of considerable strength as well as being an excellent outpost for the town of Newark which was very firmly Royalist. Whilst leading the troops into the fort, Captain Thornhalgh received a musket ball in his chest and fell dead. As the Captain was the former commander of Broxtowe fort, it was not long before the news of his death reached his old comrades. The sad tidings were speedily dispatched to Lady Agnes at Aspley Hall.

After weeping, Lady Agnes put aside all her fine clothes and lived a life of prayer and fasting, giving alms to the poor, and visiting the sick. The one thing that she was so upset about was that her lover had died a heretic, and all her prayers were for his soul that he might meet her in heaven. She never loved anyone else, but was loyal to him for the remaining 60 years of her life. When she eventually died, we are informed that she was greatly mourned by all the people for her gentle ways. Her help to those in their hours of need had done a great deal to endear her to all the people of the countryside around.

*   *   *

Another love story which has become even more than a legend is that connected with St. Catherine's Well at Newark. There were once two knights, Sir Everard Bevercotes and Sir Guy Saucimer, who both fell in love with the daughter of Alan De Caldwell. Now it seemed that the lady in question was more taken with Sir Everard, and showed him more favours. This angered Sir Guy, who slayed his rival and then went away to foreign parts. Isabell, who was Alan's daughter, died of grief. On the spot where Everard was slain a stream of pure water gushed from the ground.

It was not until he learned of the way that Isabell had died that Sir Guy decided to return to England, although since the day he had slain his rival he had been covered in leprous sores. One day, while he was sleeping in the forest of Avold, a vision of the holy Saint Catherine appeared to him. She revealed that only at the stream where he had slain his rival could his sores be healed. He then journeyed as a hermit towards the place and, having changed his name to Sir Guthred, he built himself a small dwelling place on the banks of the river Devon. He lived in this cell until he was 87 years of age and was much loved by all for his piety and goodness. The waters of St. Catherine's Well are still held in very high repute for their purity and goodness.

4. Witches and Ghosts

ONE of the best known places in Nottinghamshire is Newstead Abbey. This was the home of Lord Byron who did so much to try and support the poor, especially during the Luddite uprisings. Byron is of course much better known as a poet. Newstead Abbey has only been acquired by the Council during this century, when it was put up for sale in lots. The legends attached to the Abbey and its lake, however, live on.

Lord Byron, the poet, we think of very much as a realist, in spite of the fact that he wrote poetry and had several affairs which brought him into disrepute. On the other hand it must be stated that he was very much disliked by his contemporaries for taking the side of the working man. He was always doing his utmost to help the poor, and in the House of Lords he stood up and referred to "A Committee of Butchers" for passing the law to hang any Luddite that was found.

Byron saw the ghost of the Black Friar. This was a very old monk associated with the early days of the Abbey. It was said that he always brought bad tidings to members of the Byron Family and, as it happened, he appeared to Byron just before his marriage, which as we all know was in fact a disaster. Miss Milbanke was a very jealous woman, whose imagination often ran riot. Byron wrote that

A monk arrayed in cowl and beads and dusky garb appeared,
Now in the moonlight, now lapsed in the shade,
With steps that trod as heavy, yet unheard.

Another apparition which was greatly feared at the Abbey was that of a column of white vapour, which felt cold to the touch and was sometimes seen to rise from the floor of one of the old panelled bedrooms. This always happened at midnight.

One "ghost" of Newstead leaves a horrible question in your mind—was she a ghost, or was she real? I don't know and probably no-one ever will. This is the story of the white lady, who it is said actually lived in the grounds of Newstead at Weir Mill Farm. Colonel Wildman was the owner of the Abbey at the time, and went to great pains to find out who the girl was, and who her parents were. Her father was a bookseller and the girl's name was Sophia Hyett. After her parents died she had but a mere pittance to live on. It seems that the only thing she lived for was to see Lord Byron walking around the grounds, and when he died Colonel Wildman sent a deputation to see her and offer her a home within the Abbey grounds. As the deputation arrived, her coach was just seen leaving. It is reported that she got out of the coach at the entrance to the Abbey to see along the road. The oncoming carriage could not stop quickly enough and ran over the girl. It is supposed that her ghost haunts the Abbey grounds to this day.

*   *   *

Another sign of ill tidings was the death omen of the Clifton family. The ancient family of Cliftons, who occupied Clifton Hall well into the middle of this century, were supposed to be fore-warned of a death occurring in their family by the sight of a Royal Sturgeon swimming up the river Trent and circling around in the Grove area of the river which was actually part of their land.

*   *   *

In March 1883 a story of a poltergeist appeared in the Retford newspaper. It appears that on the 21st February a Mrs. White and two of her children were in the kitchen doing the washing up after tea. Suddenly the whole table on which they were working tipped over. Mrs. White managed to save the bowl which she was using, but the candle fell onto the floor. It all seemed rather strange at the time for Mrs. White realised that none of her children was near the table, but she gave the matter no further consideration.

The following Monday, Mr. White, who was a horse dealer by trade, had to go away for a week on business. While he was away, Mrs. White invited a girl called Rose to stay with her. It was not until about 11-30 on Thursday night that anything happened. When the children were in their bed, and their uncle Tom White had gone upstairs, Mrs. White and Rose decided to sit quietly in the kitchen for a half hour before they went to bed themselves. All of a sudden they heard queer noises coming from the stairs outside. Mrs. White and Rose went out to see what

40

was the matter, and were surprised to find crockery, which had been in the kitchen a few minutes earlier, now rolling down the stairs. Everyone in the house denied that they had anything to do with it, and when all was quiet they went to bed.

The following night, Friday, Mr. White returned home, and of course refused to believe much a peculiar story. At 11-30 that night, however, he was left in no doubt as to the truth of it, for not only did the noises start again, but this time knives and forks as well as pottery flew around, parts of the carpet flew and the noise was so great that the neighbours and the local policeman came in to find out what was the matter. They all saw for themselves the flying crockery smashing itself against the wall. Yet at 2-0 a.m. everything returned to normal. Later that day the disturbances started again, and an American clock which had not chimed for more than eighteen months began to strike the hour. It then fell onto its face on the floor. A chest of drawers turned itself upside down and was smashed. Mr. and Mrs. White were genuinely kind people, but it appeared to Mr. White that wherever Rose went, the things just seemed to fly about, and so kindly and gently he asked her to leave. After she had left the house nothing more happened.

*　　*　　*

In a very poor house near Rempstone lived a lad by the name of Jack, with his mother. In order to earn a few pence that he and his mother might live, every day Jack went to a nearby farm to beg the buttermilk after the butter had been churned. This milk he sold to neighbouring villages as food for their pigs or cattle. In one village there lived a witch, and one day she asked Jack for some buttermilk, but he refused to give her any. She then asked again, threatening that if he refused once more she would put him into her sack and carry him into her house. Now in those days witches were very much feared, and no-one refused anyone who was even suspected of witchcraft. Jack, however, being so poor, realised that giving the buttermilk to the witch would leave both his mother and himself to starve. So again he refused. The witch carried out her threat and pushed him into her sack. Part of the way along the road she realised that she had left a pot of fat in the village, and seeing two men cutting the hedge she left the sack in their care.

When she had gone Jack called out to the startled men. "If you will let me out," he cried, "and help me fill this sack with thorns, I will give you some buttermilk." This they did, and then they parted company.

The tale of Jack, a poor boy of Rempstone, who successfully outwitted a witch.

When the witch returned she picked up the sack, and gradually the thorns started to stick in her. "Jack," she said "thou hast got some pins about thee lad." When she arrived home, she lay a white sheet on the floor and tipped out the sack. On seeing all the thorns she became very angry. "I'll catch thee tomorrow and boil thee, Jack" she shouted.

The next day the witch met Jack again, and again he refused to give her the buttermilk, so he was put into the sack once more. This time she remembered that she had left some eggs in the village, so she left the sack with the road mender. Jack pleaded with the road mender as he had done with the hedge cutters, and this time they filled the bag with stones. Soon afterwards the witch returned and continued on her way home. The stones began to chink together, and she called out, "My word Jack, thy bones do crack." When she reached home she got out the sheet as before, and on seeing the stones she swore to get him the following day.

The witch found Jack again the following day, and yet again he refused her his buttermilk and was bundled into the sack. This time he was not so lucky for the witch carried him straight home and locked him into her kitchen. Fortunately Jack had a knife in his pocket and, while the witch went outside to collect the herbs and vegetables to boil him in, he very quietly cut his way out of the sack. He then collected all the crockery from inside the kitchen and placed it in the sack, so that one could not see where the sack had been cut. Quickly he climbed up the chimney and was away over the rooftops before the witch returned. When she did come back and emptied the sack, breaking all her crockery, she was so angry that she vowed she would never attempt to catch Jack again.

Ever since the beginning of time people have been interested in ghosts and witchcraft. Many were the witch hunts which took place in the centuries gone by. I must confess that I am a devout coward, who has a completely open mind upon the subject, nor I must also confess have I any wish to find out for myself.

*　　*　　*

People who travel regularly between Nottingham and Mansfield will know the Bessie Stone which stands close to Harlow Wood Hospital. The stone is not now as noticeable as it was in years gone by, for it stands in a dip as a result of improvements which have been made to the road at this point. In fact it is a monument to a girl who died nearly 160 years ago. An inscription states that "It is erected to the memory of Elizabeth Shepherd of Papplewick who was murdered on this spot by Charles Rotherham on July 7th, 1817." There are several versions as to the murderer's capture. One says that he was caught on the way to Loughborough, while standing leaning over a bridge gazing into the water. Another says that he was caught in Mansfield having sold the girl's shoes in Nottingham Market, and another that he sold the shoes in Mansfield Market and was caught in Nottingham. Anway, he was caught and hanged in Nottingham. It was not long afterwards that the girl's apparition was first seen on the spot, and coach drivers often reported seeing her. Eventually they came to the conclusion that whenever her gravestone was disturbed she would appear. The stone was struck by a passing car in 1956 and it was not long afterwards that her ghost was seen by a young couple returning home along that road. The apparition was described as being of medium height with a long flowing robe. She hovered over the stone for a little while and then disappeared.

* * *

The fear of witchcraft it seems is much greater than the fear of ghosts. In fact this area has very few recordings of witchcraft, and yet the fear of witches was enough to make full grown men shake in their shoes. There is one very well-known story of a shoemaker, who lived in the north of the county and was in terrible fear of witches and wizards. He stood well over six feet tall, and was so strong that he would often demonstrate his ability to dance while fully dressed in a suit of armour or chain mail. On the front of his door he had many horse shoes securely fastened, but vowed that even these were insufficient to keep him from the spells of the witches and wizards of the surrounding area. In order to combat their spells he kept beside his fire a sack which was full of salt. This he mixed with the cast-off nails from the horse shoes and the nails which he bent while continuing with his trade. On particularly dark or stormy nights, he would stay awake continually throwing handfuls of this mixture onto the fire, while praying to the Lord to torment all witches and devils that their spells might have no effect. All night the fire was kept burning with a purple hue. During the day he would occasionally carry out this same ritual. Someone at sometime must have doubted the man's sanity, for it is reported that on being questioned about his behaviour he was pronounced as a good God-fearing man who was also grave and sober.

In many Nottinghamshire villages you can still see the horse shoes nailed onto the doors to bring the householder good luck.

It is a superstition which remains with us, and is the reason why horse shoes made out of paper are found in the bags of confetti used at a wedding. They are to bring luck and prosperity to the happy couple as well as to ward off evil spirits.

*　　*　　*

Although Nottinghamshire had very little witchcraft or witch hunting, unlike many other areas in the country, the fear of witches was just as great as elsewhere. On the whole the days of witch hunts were very few in Nottingham, but when they were found they were treated just as roughly as elsewhere, even if it was proved they were tricksters playing upon the fears of the local people. There were, however, many superstitious remedies for ailments which would be laughed at today, and certainly they had no basis at all in the world of medical science.

One remedy which we would all find extremely funny today was the olden days' cure for whooping cough. For this some hair was cut from the back of the head of the child suffering from the disease, and this was placed between two slices of buttered bread. The parent then had to go out into the street and give this to the first dog to be seen. If the dog ate it straight away the parent could expect to return home to find the child cured. It was believed that the cure was immediately effective. It now seems strange, but this belief was still current in Nottingham a hundred years ago.

Oh, the rapturous way they described tea a century ago! It was classed as "the cup that cheers but not inebriates" and was much appreciated, but also had superstitions attached to it. If a stalk was found floating in the tea cup, it was supposed to indicate the approach of a sweetheart or a stranger. The time of his or her arrival could be discovered by placing the stem on the back of the hand and smacking it with the back of the other hand. The number of blows indicated the number of days which were to pass before the arrival. As soon as the stalk was transferred to the other hand the counting stopped.

Cats were always kept well away from children. There was some idea that a cat, if allowed near a young child, would catch its breath. In fact this may have been the very beginning of people's realisation that the hair of animals could cause such diseases as asthma, about which at that time very little if anything was known. Certainly there were sound reasons for keeping a cat out of a baby's cot, for cats love warmth and many deaths have been caused by a cat sleeping on the face of a child and smothering it. In many cases, however, the cat was not even

45

allowed in the same room.

One present which was usually given to a child soon after its birth was a well-known Nottingham toy with rings, bells and a piece of coral on the end. This was generally suspended from the neck by a piece of coloured ribbon. The original meaning of this gift was that the coral prevented anyone bewitching the child, while the bells were supposed to preserve the child from evil spirits. This explanation of the gift goes right back into the early days of witchcraft.

Sherwood Legends

MANY people looked upon the trees within the forest of Sherwood as being immortal, and indeed they must have seemed so, for where our lives might be expected to be counted in tens of years the trees' lives could be counted in hundreds. More especially was this so because the majority of the trees in Sherwood were in fact oaks and grew to an enormous size and age. I have heard many visitors express their disappointment at the present size of Sherwood Forest, and this must seem to them a very little forest when compared with the days of the legendary Robin Hood. What most people forget to take into account is the fact that England is now much more highly populated than it was in those days, and that we have also had the industrial revolution and coal mining brought onto the scene, for which both labour and houses were required. For these reasons trees were cut down fairly extensively, and the forests which once covered the whole of central England have now dwindled to a few hundred acres. Fire, too, has played its part in the destruction of the forest, but nevertheless we do have at least some of it left to remind us of days gone by.

Perhaps the most famous tree is the Parliament Oak. Here again, because of lack of real knowledge, the tree is associated with two kings, firstly King John. One very popular belief is that, while he was hunting in the forest, word was brought to him of an uprising of the Welsh people. So he summoned Parliament under this tree to consider what should be done. It stands on the high ground on the borders of Nottinghamshire and Derbyshire, and thus was a tree which could be fairly easily found. The result of this Parliament was supposed to have been that instructions were issued by King John to take prisoner 200 Welsh boys and brings them as slaves to Nottingham Castle. The other story concerns Edward I, who was on his way to Scotland in 1290 and had summoned a Parliament to meet at Clipston. The proceedings opened on St. Michael's Day, but there is no record of what the assembly was about, although it is quite likely that a meeting of some sort did in fact take place.

Another tree which has kept its fame over the years is

Hooton's Oak, or the Butcher's Shambles. When it was discovered the whole of the inside of the tree had been hollowed out, and in its place were rails and hooks on which to hang meat and game. When the tree was found it was well stocked with venison and game from the king's forests. Hooton was another outlaw and he managed his escape among the greenwood trees. In those days there were many outlaws in the forest and one reads of sheriffs and abbots bing robbed of much money and church plate, but there are no records I have managed to discover that give undeniable proof as to who did the robbing.

The remains of the Pilgrims' Oak can be seen just outside the gates of Newstead Abbey, the famous home of Lord Byron which is now a museum to his memory. When the Abbey really was an abbey, it was here outside the gates that the pilgrims used to meet.

The Major Oak, as it is now called, is reached by the footpath which starts at the Edwinstowe corner of the forest. It was once known at the Queen's Oak, but it was re-named in 1806 after a Major Rooke. The tree is 30 feet in circumference, although many of its heavier boughs now have to be supported by chains.

Another tree which reached enormous proportions was that at Welbeck Abbey known as the Greendale Oak. This tree was so large that the owner of the Abbey, the Earl of Oxford, had a bet with some of his friends that a hole could be made through the tree sufficiently large to take a carriage and pair as if it was merely an arch. The bet was made and taken up. The wood from the centre of the tree was given to the Countess of Oxford, who had a writing cabinet made from the wood. The hole was large enough and the Earl won his bet, but unfortunately a few years showed that the whole idea had been a complete failure as far as the tree was concerned for it died. When the remains of the tree were demolished, because it had begun to get dangerous, there was found to be more than nine tons of wood left in the trunk.

In the early 19th century there was a custom that the farmers on the edge of Sherwood Forest would have a celebration if all the wheat had been sown by Martinmas, November 11th. The labourers would be given hopper cake and ale. This meant that all the wheat which had been left was ground into flour and, when an ordinary dough had been made, fat and seeds were added and the whole was baked upon the hearth. In 1894 there were thoughts of reviving this custom, but it was never recorded as to whether anyone did or not.

*   *   *

Welbeck Abbey's Greendale Oak, through which the Earl of Oxford successfully drove a carriage and pair as the result of a wager.

The crags at Cresswell, which lie to the west of Sherwood on the borders of Nottinghamshire and Derbyshire, are well known to archaeologists but far less familiar to the man in the street. The first thing one notices is that the stone is an unusual one for it is magnesian limestone, and this is in fact the same stone that has been used for the building of the Houses of Parliament. In a less polluted atmosphere it is a very good building material and it may be seen today in the nave of Southwell Minster. At Cresswell a running stream has carved out a long ravine, so that on each side are the steep limestone cliffs and the caverns which were explored for the first time in about 1890. The early scientists were amazed at the bones which they found. These included such animals as bison, lions, tigers, hyenas, arctic fox and elephant. Many of the bones were reported to have been gnawed in the way usually expected of hyenas. Another very important find to the scientists was a milk tooth belonging to a mammoth. This was one which could complete the set already in the British Museum.

One of these caves has a very old custom attached to it. It is called the Pin Hole Cave. As each person enters he or she should put down a pin, and pick one up. This is supposed to bring the traveller good luck. Another of these caves is called Mother Grundy's Pantry, and it was here that most of the bone finds were made.

6. Legends from Town and Village

CLIFTON village, its green and its grove were for generations the scenes of frivolity, especially on Sunday afternoons during the summer months. The people of the village were not slow to take commercial advantage of this, and teas were served in the cottages and on the lawns outside. From Nottingham the young people would take the ferry to Wilford and walk along the grove to the village. They would often bring with them musical instruments of all sorts. Deering, an historian of the 18th century, writes of the young people tripping the light fantastic over the village green. The teas which were served were mostly boiled eggs or local-grown fruit as and when it was in season. Deering writes of the people not returning to the town until the light was fading, and that their merry laughter could be heard in the village long after they left as they helped each other over the stiles. They then returned across the river on the ferry.

Clifton was one of the earliest villages in Nottinghamshire, and was in fact one of those mentioned in the Domesday Book, yet it had no ferry of its own until the middle of the 19th century. This too had some peculiar customs which went with it. The ferryman was paid the normal fare by each individual who crossed the river, but at Christmas the villagers had to supply him with the finest white loaf obtainable. His Christmas dinner had to be supplied to him by the vicar, the ferryman eating with him at the table. What is more, the vicar's dog had to be shut out for the day in order that the ferryman's dog should be able to eat in the same house as his master and be warm and comfortable!

*   *   *

Another place where there were fun and games during the summer months was at St. Ann's Well. Right until the middle of the last century, there was a long walk comprising nothing but green fields separating Nottingham from the old well. This was

actually situated at the back of where The Gardeners public
house is now, although the water from the well has been culverted into the Beck and from there into the Trent. The water
of St. Ann's Well was well known all over England for its ability
to restore the sexual powers of the people who drank it. Of
course, there were one or two items of commerce which grew
up beside the well. One of these was an inn; there was a maze;
and a museum dedicated to the memory of Robin Hood. After a
time many complaints were made by the townsfolk about the
bawdy goings on as the people returned after dark and entered
the town. Eventually the case was brought before the city magis-
trates, who ordered the inn to be closed by law. It was then
decided that the inn should be turned into a tea house. This,
however, proved a financial disaster right from the start, and
eventually the owners became bankrupt.

The museum really did not prove such a tremendous attraction
after the start, for so many of the so called relics were obviously
not what they were supposed to be. For example, there was a
tooth there which was reputed to have come from Robin's head,
and it was about the size of a small elephant tusk! There were
other specimens, too, such as his bow and arrow and his hat,
but it was objects like the tooth which cast permanent doubt as
to the honesty of all the rest. Now, with all the water culverted,
there is very little chance of finding out whether it had any
aphrodisiac qualities, but certainly the whole place was enjoyed
by many of the populace for quite a long period of time.

There was another custom associated with St. Ann's Well
which, Deering informs us, goes back further than any living
memory. This was visiting the Woodward of the Well to pay
homage, the visit being made by the Mayor and all the Corporation, Aldermen and Burgesses, accompanied by their wives.
This ceremony would take place each Easter Monday after
prayers, the procession being preceded by the town waits who
played their music. As it was Easter everyone was sure to be
dressed in their finest regalia, providing a happy spectacle for
the people of the town. The Woodward of the Well was in fact
the chief forester of the area, and it was his responsibility of
keeping sufficient wood stocked up for the town's use each winter.
After paying their homage the procession then returned home.

*   *   *

In the middle of a field close to Berry Hill, near Mansfield,
there used to be an old tumble-down cottage, known years ago
as Whitehead's Folly. The story of its coming into being goes

back between two and three hundred years when the town had rather a severe outbreak of smallpox. A man whose name was Whitehead, and who owned this particular field, was so terrified of catching the disease that he had this building erected so that he could go and live there away from anyone else. Unfortunately his well-laid plans were not to be, for the woman who brought his bed unwittingly carried the disease into the house. He died entirely alone as a result and was not found until after his death.

The plague was another disease which caused an immense amount of suffering in those days, and people would leave their homes and wander the country hoping to avoid the terrible disease. This was one of the main reasons that all strangers were suspect, for they could be carrying the disease on their clothing, or have actually contracted it, and if they had money would put up in a town, quickly infecting hundreds of others. Therefore the law that no strangers were to be allowed into a town was the only means the people knew of protecting themselves. The poor, however, generally remained in the forests, hunting and finding what food they could.

In 1665 many people found their way into the forest where they set up a camp near East Retford. The country people would have nothing to do with the visitors, but were unwilling to see them suffer more than was necessary. It took some time before arrangements were made, and until that time the people in the wood were sorely troubled for the winter had come and they were almost dying of starvation. Then a barter system was worked out between those in the village of East Retford and those in the forest. It was arranged from a distance that the people would in the morning place the money for goods they needed on a broad stone which was at the side of the road. Several hours later someone from the village would come and collect the money, and leave the goods required in its place. Gradually, this came to be called the Breadstone for the money and the food were all placed on it. The stone was a considerable distance from the town. The people of the forest were grateful to the country people of East Retford, for they had come a long way from London, and had been poorly treated by most of the towns and villages along the way.

*   *   *

How many times Mansfield Gooseberry Pork Pie was mentioned to me before I was actually able to find out about it, I cannot think, but it turns out to be a gooseberry pie made in the same casing as one would normally use for a pork pie. It was customary for this special pie to be prepared for the July fair, and also for the Oxton Feast. Usually it would be cooked by individual housewives, but there were occasions when it was made in a very large size and was carved for the Mayor and the Corporation as well as the children of the town. One of these occasions was in 1927 on July 15th when a foot-high pie weighing 70 lbs. was made to celebrate the charter which was given to the town of Mansfield by Richard II in 1377.

Various hotels and cafes laid on wonderful meals for their customers on that day, and spent the whole of the previous day in spit roasting whole sides of beef and other delectable items. The meals were given free to well known customers of different shops, and this of course encouraged them to continue to shop at the same place. On the other hand, in order to get these vast quantities of food ready, whole factories and bakeries had to be taken over the day before the fair in order to cook the potatoes and other vegetables which were required. In general it was a fair which was very much enjoyed by rich and poor alike in Mansfield, and those who probably enjoyed it then more than anyone else were the children—as indeed they do today.

Another custom which was kept up in King's Mill long after it had been forgotten in Mansfield was that of "going a-gooding" on St. Thomas's Day. The older people would go, with the poor, to the principal houses in the district begging for provisions, or indeed for the money to buy them with, just before Christmas. In return for the goods or money given to them, the poor people would give sprigs of holly or mistletoe in return. In the very early years it was always called "going a-Thomassing". The change of name seems to have taken place during the puritanical era.

*   *   *

On the main road going into Mansfield from Nottingham you can see Forest Road on your right hand side. On the corner there is an empty space where a public house called Ye Leather Bottell once stood. In the first place it was a snug, cottage-like residence standing back from the road. Few people realise that it was at one time a hostelry and that for almost three centuries it was the last house on the road before you came to The Hutt at Newstead. It was therefore a favourite place for travellers. Here they could stay for food, rest and refreshments before starting their long walk into Nottingham through the forest. It seems that for several years a family by the name of Martyn kept the place. As all the country around was forest, the actual road to Nottingham ran over the place where the cemetery now stands. In the centre of the road there was once a large stone on which was carved in old English characters,

John Martyn's stone I am,
Shows ye great roade to Nottyngham,
    1621.

There was a good reason why Ye Leather Bottell was closed, and the story of the mishap dates from the end of the last century. It was a very cold and stormy night when a man carrying the king's mail set out for Mansfield. The journey from Nottingham had to be made on foot passing through the forest. As he left Nottingham behind him the storm began to increase in its intensity, and snow drifts had made parts of the road impassable. It was late when he reached The Hutt. He was weary, footsore and almost frozen, but he could afford only a short time to rest if he was to finish his journey. By this time the storm was at the height of its fury, but he plodded his way along and was very relieved when he saw Ye Leather Bottell come into sight, and could see the great guide stone still visible in the snow. Eventually he arrived at the inn, and almost crawled to the door. By this time he was almost totally exhausted. He knocked and demanded refreshment in the king's name as the bearer of the king's mail. The landlord, however, refused him admittance and told him to go where the climate is supposed to be more warm than desirable. The poor postman had then to make yet another effort to reach Mansfield, but the cold and exhaustion had done their work and the next morning the people of Mansfield were horrified to hear that the body of Postman Baggaley had been found dead near the water meadows. This area is now known as Titchfield Park. He was frozen to death, but still firmly clutching the bags containing the king's mail.

There was an enormous crowd present at the funeral. When it came to the ears of the justices of Mansfield, that the landlord of Ye Leather Bottell had refused to allow him warmth and refreshments, a special meeting was held. This sitting decided that the house should be closed as an inn for ever. It was then bought as private property and eventually became derelict. There are, I understand, relatives of Postman Baggaley still living in the Mansfield area.

Among the purely Mansfield traditions is the fact that they always used to call a black cat Dennis. In the very early part of the 19th century the local sweep for the Mansfield area was a man by the name of Dennis. He was known far and wide in the area as being an eccentric character. No-one can be really sure, but the general concensus of opinion seems to be that it was after him that the Mansfield people named their cats. He died somewhere around 1819. His wife died in 1832, and it was then that someone was heard to remark that she was the widow of Dennis, the sweep, after whom all the cats were named.

*   *   *

"All the world and Bingham" is a phrase which was once very much in common use. The way that the saying came into being goes back to the early days of the railways. On a noticeboard posted on a hostelry in Newark, which was a great centre for carriers, there was painted an advertisement bearing the words: "Passengers and Parcels Conveyed to all parts of the world—and to Bingham". This innocently written notice seemed to imply that Bingham was not part of this world, but had a separate being of its own, which of course caused a great deal of merriment to all concerned.

An historian of olden days by the name of Echard, when writing about Newark, tells us that the women of that town were obedient to their husbands. This he attributed to the number of queens who had at one time or another resided in Newark; their instant obedience to the king had set such a good example to the women that they copied it.

*   *   *

In 1710 "The Tatler", a newspaper which existed then, wrote of complaints sent to London by the ladies of Nottingham. The cause of these complaints was the lack of sleep, which was disturbed nightly by certain riotous lovers who during the summer had infested the streets of the town between the hours of twelve and four each night. They were playing violins and bass-violas. Although they were supposed to serenade the young women, they caused so much annoyance that "good honest citizens" had become enraged at the noise and had taken to throwing things.

Another type of serenading which took place in Nottingham was performed by the butchers of the town by banging their meat cleavers on marrow bones. One such serenade was performed on the return of Mr. D. P. Coke after he had been elected Member of Parliament. The butchers did the job in style, too, for they all wore blue waistcoats. So proud were they of their accomplishment that they followed the Member around the town and performed in the Market Place and again in the Corn

The serenading butchers of Nottingham who performed by banging their meat cleavers on marrow bones.

Market. They were then sent for by a lady, Mrs. Pole of Radbourne, who requested them to play another peal outside her lodgings, and for this paid them a guinea and a half. By grinding their cleavers eight men could produce a perfect octave. They started to perform for weddings and other celebrations, and usually were paid for their services. For weddings they all wore blue aprons and had a white paper either in their breast pockets or in their hats. If it seemed that no fee would be forthcoming they did not leave, but carried on making more and more noise until as can be imagined the people paid up to get rid of them.

*　　*　　*

A marriage custom which lasted for many years was the one in the village of Wellow. When the banns of marriage were read in the church it was customary for one of the clerks to stand and say, "God speed them well". The clerk and the congregation responded "Amen".

It was also the privilege of sweeps in the Nottingham area to levy "blackmail" onto all couples about to get married. Should the demand not be met, "the knight of the brush" would threaten to shake his bag of soot all over the intending bride as she left the house to go to the church on her wedding day. In order to prevent this the demand was usually complied with, with the best wishes of the local chimney sweep. In North Nottinghamshire an old boot used to be placed on the vehicle taking the bride to the church. This encouraged the luck to go with the couple instead of it following after them. Also in the same area there used to be a tradition of throwing rice or wheat over the happy pair. This was said to bring domestic happiness and a large family. As the corn was thrown, the words said were "bread for life and pudding forever".

Going from one extreme to another, it was always considered a good thing if it rained on the coffin at a funeral. This was supposed to be a sign that the soul had gone to heaven. The actual expression used was, "Blessed is the dead that the rain falls on".

*　　*　　*

No doubt you have either heard or read of Mary Chaworth's love for Byron, but of course through being cousins they were not allowed to get married. The actual man whom Mary Chaworth married was Squire Musters of Colwick Hall. He was a very jealous man, and was cruel to Mary. Colwick Hall was only saved during the Parliamentary Reform riots because someone put a feather mattress on top of the burning timbers, causing them only to smoulder until the rioting crowd had left the place. Squire Musters was hated by everyone, for he was a most severe magistrate, his punishments being the hardest possible.

When he was at home he kept guard over his stretch of the river Trent, and yet it was here that he showed his most eccentric form. "Ho! Young fellow," he would cry on seeing a youngster poaching, "tell me what paper does your father read?" If the reply was that the paper was The Journal, the youngster could fish all day in peace. If by any chance it happened to be The Review, the Squire immediately lost his temper, shouted to the lad to depart instantly and chased him off with a whip. It was not long before the word got round among the youngsters, and it really must have been quite surprising how many radical parents nominally took the conservative Journal!

*   *   *

A village which is now virtually lost in antiquity is that of Scrooby in the north of the county, and yet this tiny place has left a great mark on the world. From here came many of the Pilgrim Fathers, who eventually set sail in the "Mayflower" and did a great deal to populate America. Scrooby was in the early days the seat of the Archbishops of York. It lay between Retford and Bawtry, with the tiny river Ryton separating the two sides of the village street. At one end of the street the river was spanned by a watermill, the ancient stones of which bear the names of people who carved them way back in 1710. When Thoroton wrote of this village he compared the Archbishop's Palace here with that at Southwell and said that it was better provided for. In the Domesday Book it is entered as the Archbishop of York's Manor; it was then only a few cottages and one or two big houses, and of course the Palace.

Gradually the flock known as the Pilgrim Fathers began to grow, although it was not approved of by James I, and meetings were held in the outbuildings. Deputations were made to James who eventually allowed the Fathers to build their own ship, the "Mayflower", which sailed for America on August 5th, 1620, from Southampton.

Many Americans still visit the site of the old village to see where their ancestors lived—famous names like Brewster; John Smythe and Richard Clifton, both of whom were ministers in the

The Pilgrim Fathers, who set sail in the "Mayflower" for America, came from the Nottinghamshire village of Scrooby.

church as it stood; William Bradford; and the Rev. John Robinson, whose name has been passed down to posterity as being closely connected with the settlement of New England. In Virginia the Governor was Sir Edmund Sandys, who was the brother of the owner of Scrooby, and was Brewster's old landlord. It is still possible to see the vague outline of the old village, although after the Fathers left it was divided into farmland. The Palace was pulled apart, while the remainder was allowed to decay. There is a stone dedicated to Penelope Sandys in the floor of the church, firmly linking Scrooby with America.

Legendary Characters

WAY back in 1722, there lived in Warsop one Thomas Smith, who was the owner and landlord of the White Lion Inn. He was a real character in the village, being full of spirit as well as being very small in height. It was because of these two factors that the village knew him as Tommy Tit. A story is told of this little man which eventually gave rise to a proverb in Warsop.

One Sunday morning a traveller called at the White Lion for a pint of ale. As Tommy was not about, his wife served him with the ale and showed him into the parlour, where a pot was boiling on the hearth with their Sunday dinner in it. While her back was turned, the man lifted the lid of the pot, abstracted a dumpling and then quietly made off with it. The wife, on coming back into the room, went to the pot to attend to the meal and discovered that the dumpling, which was her husband's favourite tit-bit, had gone. After Mrs. Smith had informed Tommy what had happened, he immediately ran after the culprit and, on catching him, flew at him in a terrible temper and knocked him down. A neighbour who was passing at the time, and could not help but be amused at the scene, asked him, "What is the matter, Thomas?"

"Matter enough," came the reply, and pointing to his favourite tit-bit he continued "it's a poor dog that won't fight for his own dumpling".

*   *   *

John Stubbins was the son of a sawyer on the Warsop Estate. John enlisted in the Dragoon Guards, where he rose to the rank of corporal and took part with his regiment to overthrow Napoleon at the Battle of Waterloo. It was on this occasion that he greatly distinguished himself in hand-to-hand fighting with the French soldiers. During one of these encounters John Stubbins's horse had an ear cut off by the sabre of a Frenchman and he himself only just escaped being wounded. After the battle was over, John was promoted to sergeant. The following year he retired from the army and was presented with £20 and a medal for the part he had played in bringing England to victory. The medal was, and I believe still is, treasured by his family. Strange to say, the thing which impressed the people of the area so much happened two years after John had retired. For some reason a detachment of his old regiment had cause to pass through Warsop, and with it came John's old horse. The detachment halted in front of the Hare and Hounds. The meeting of the two was reported as being most touching, and the whole village turned out to see the one-eared horse that John Stubbins rode at Waterloo.

*　　*　　*

Most people will have heard of the miller and the king in Mansfield. This was eventually written as a very popular play by Robert Dodsley, "The King and the Miller of Mansfield", which was performed at the Theatre Royal in Drury Lane. This is of course one reason for the continued popularity of the legend— one which no book on Nottinghamshire folk lore should be without. For some reason the king quoted in several recent story books is named as Henry VIII, but in truth it is more likely that it was Henry II. For there are no records of Henry VIII ever having come to Nottingham, never mind having hunted there. Henry II did however come to Nottingham quite often, and hunting was one of his chief pleasures. I think we may be reasonably sure that the king in this case was Henry II.

The legend tells us how the king was out hunting with his nobles one evening in Sherwood Forest, and as it got dark the king found himself separated from the rest of his party. While seeking for a path by which he could return to Nottingham, he met a miller, one John Cockle, and stopped to ask him the way. The miller mistook the king for a gentleman robber, and it took the king a great deal of talking to convince John Cockle that he was neither a thief nor a runaway. He explained his clothes by saying that he was a courtier. John then took the king home with him, and after explaining that he would have to share a bed with his son, for which he would provide fresh straw and clean hempen sheets, invited him to take supper with him. While his wife made the supper, John assisted the king with the feeding, bedding down and grooming of his horse.

The supper which was served was that of hot-bag puddings and apple pie. They followed this with some meat pasties which were made with venison. The king was extremely hungry, and

63

told them that he had never tasted food so dainty and good
before, and naturally asked what it was. The son replied that
it was their daily food, and that it was venison from the forest.
They then made Henry keep it a secret, for they knew they could
be beheaded if the king found out. The next day the nobles were
out early looking for their king, and it was fortunate that as
they came to the miller's house the king came out and was about
to mount his horse. The nobles got off their horses and knelt
before the king. The miller trembled and shook when he realised
who he had entertained the previous night. He dropped to his
knees, expecting to be decapitated at any moment. This however
was not the case for King Henry knighted Sir John Cockle, and
bestowed upon him a good living. After the king returned to
London, he sent for the miller and his wife, and also his bed-
fellow Richard, as he desired to have them at court. He increased
their living to £300 a year, but made them promise not to steal
his deer in the future. He then appointed Sir John the Over
seer to Sherwood Forest.

*　　*　　*

It was while Edward III was at Nottingham Castle that he
passed a most important piece of legislation through Parliament
which was to make a difference to the country not only at that
time but ever since. He gave assent to an Act whereby in the
future the British people would have to make and weave their
own materials. In this way he was the first man to put us on
the road to being an industrial nation. In order to achieve his
aims, he invited Flemish weavers into the country to teach the
British people how to weave. They came here by way of Norwich,
and there were for ever known as Strangers. In fact one of the
most exclusive clubs in Norwich is Strangers' Hall.

It was one of the habits of Charles I to walk around the towns
that he was visiting. One day when he was in Southwell he went
into the shop of a shoemaker, whose name was James Lee.
Finding himself unrecognised, the king asked Lee to measure
him up for a pair of shoes. No sooner had the shoemaker taken
the foot in his hand than he went into the most dreadful panic
and could not continue. When asked why he would not go on,
Lee told of a dream he had had the previous night, and this he
swore was the foot. Nought but ill could come to this man, he
told the king, and all who worked for him would not thrive.
The king himself, being very superstitious, especially after all the
misfortunes which had already befallen him, spoke some ejacu-
lation and retired from the shop.

A character who was well known both in Mansfield and in Nottingham at the end of the last century was a little man known as the Dagging Top Dwarf. His actual name was Thomas Garrod and he was born in 1852. He, like many other characters of his time, had become famous because of his continual appearance at fairs and markets. He had not been born in the area, but actually had been brought up in Stowe in Suffolk. Unfortunately not only was he very small in stature, but he had been born without any hands. When writing about his childhood days he tells how he was a favourite among his classmates, and how it was they who first lent him their whip and top and taught him as much as they could about how to spin it. He tells us that at that time he never dreamt that this was to be his way of earning a living. He used to sit in the market place on his piece of oilcloth or carpet, demonstrating his skill. Those who would challenge him were very few and far between for there was no doubt that the unfortunate dwarf had become a master of the only craft he could manage.

*   *   *

Another character of the last century was William Parker of Ruddington. When times were very hard in the framework knitters' trade, he formed the factory which he owned in Ruddington into one of the first Co-operatives in the area. Such was the energy and spirit of this man, that when he was around 90 years of age he would often go out for a day's cycling. A trip to Boston and back was not considered too far by him, and many worried for him as the roads were nothing like they are today and the tyres of his bike were solid. He nearly did come to grief on one occasion, for he fell into a thorn bush and was caught fast by the hair in his beard. Fortunately he had in his pocket a knife with which he cut himself free—this must have been a painful business to say the least. When he died, the whole village turned out to mourn him. Now under a private Trust, the old cottages and knitting shop are being renovated and turned into a museum in Ruddington.

The knitting frame was one of the biggest bones of contention during the industrial revolution. One of the men who designed and made the machine was named Heathcoat. The men who did damage had a huge price on their heads and were known as Luddites. Although they smashed the frames, there was very little bloodshed at all in Nottingham. Many people must have known at least one person who was involved, but it is amazing to be able to state that, with half the people in Nottingham either almost starving or very close to it, no one reported anything at all. We do not know how it happened, but most people believed that Heathcoat was in his factory when the Luddites raided it. In order to prevent them having to kill him, for he had recognised some of the men concerned, he was kidnapped and taken to South Devon, where he once more started up a factory which was to bring a rivalry with the Nottingham industry in later years.

*　　*　　*

There is an old Nottingham saying, when someone cannot afford to pay for something, to ask the shopkeeper to put it on the slate for him until payday. From the middle of the 1700s it was common for the chimney breasts of all public houses to be made of slate. At the end of each evening the publican would mark up on this how much each customer owed him. In Warsop there lived a man called Robert Hooke, who was noted as being a very whimsical character as well as a practical joker. He used to visit the Hare and Hounds regularly, and one day when he went in at lunch time he found that the landlord had employed a new barmaid. Realising the potential of this, he scolded her most harshly, telling her what a slut she must be to have left the previous night's scores on the slate without cleaning it for the new day. The barmaid, frightened to lose her job, immediately fetched a wet rag and cleaned the slate. On another occasion he bet a customer that he could drink an exact pennyworth of ale out of a tankard. Now this was no easy feat, for a tankard of ale cost sevenpence. The customer paid for the tankard, and placed it before Robert. He drank the whole lot, and then throwing down the penny he had bet, said: "Never mind, this is one I don't mind losing. Goodbye, old fellow!" And with that he left.

*　　*　　*

Sir Thomas Parkyns was born at the end of the 17th century, and he inherited Bunny Hall and all the estates. He was exceedingly well educated for that time, and went to school at Westminster and then on to Cambridge. Over one thing he was a fanatic, for he loved wrestling and published a book about it entitled "The Inn Play, or The Cornish Hugg Wrestler". It was supposed to give full directions on how to break all holds and

66

most falls mathematically. It went to three editions, the last of which was published in 1727, and was "sold by Humph. Wainright of Bunney". Many of the phrases in the book were written in Latin, and many of these he had inscribed on various buildings all over the village. Another curious thing was that he collected stone coffins, and was eventually buried in one of these. Before he died, however, the baronet caused his own monument to be carved and placed opposite his own pew in the chancel of the local church. This was, he stated, "so that he could look upon it every Lord's Day and ask, what is life?"

*   *   *

There is a record in the Tower of London of a pardon which was granted to Cecilia Ridgeway, who at the Assizes in Nottingham refused to plead guilty to the murder of her husband. She was remanded back into prison, where it was recorded she went for forty days without either food or drink. This was regarded as such a miracle that she received a pardon under the Great Seal of England. As this incident happened in the early 14th century, it is understandable that it was seen as a sign from God that the woman was in the right.

*   *   *

Practically every history book on Nottingham refers somewhere to Dr. Deering, who wrote extensively and very truthfully on the events which had preceded him as well as those which happened in his lifetime. He died in 1749, a time when very few people could read and there was therefore very little sale for his books except to the rich. When a lady named Mrs. Turner heard of the historian's severe illness and his poverty she took herself to visit him. After conversing with him for some time, and seeing for herself the state that he was in, she left half a guinea with the mistress of the house to be used for his needs. When he found out about the gift he said, "I would that you would have stabbed me to the heart, for this I cannot bear."

*   *   *

Before the present Council House was built in front of the Market Square in Nottingham, the main building was known as the Exchange and it stood for 200 years before it was finally demolished. Mr. Woolley who resided at Codnor, was identified with this building as the maker and donor of the clock. When Mr. Woolley was young he was caught shooting on an estate, and he vowed there and then that he would never stop working until he had enough land to justify him taking part in his favourite sport on his own grounds. Accordingly he set to work and toiled both day and night, even denying himself a proper bed. Only the very meanest of his needs would he spend money on. Once he had gained all the money he needed, he found that he was no longer interested in shooting, and so he continued in his trade, only leaving it at odd times in order to buy and sell land. Eventually he really had amassed quite a fortune, and when he died he left this to a relative.

A story told about him shows just how mean he had become. One Sunday a man called to pay for a clock which Mr. Woolley had completed. He was asked if he would like to stay for a meal, and the man agreed. "Well then," came the reply, "I will boil a whole penny loaf; otherwise I should only have cooked half a one." This he did over a cow dung fire, and it formed the whole meal for the two of them!

8. Plays and Games

THIS is a very old play which used to be performed in the Mansfield area around Christmas time. I am greatly indebted to Mr. Mellors of Mansfield, whose research several years ago uncovered it, and for his permission for me to reproduce it here. Mansfield was always a small town, and this play we must presume was an elementary form of pantomime. The men would perform in public houses as well as in the houses of the gentry. The custom was still alive in the 1860s but since then has faded away altogether until now it is impossible even to obtain a copy of the words.

Entitled "Poor owd 'oss", it is of course partly in dialect, but to alter it into basic English would I feel be wrong and would in fact spoil the play. The "owd 'oss" was performed by a man who was draped in a dark cloth. The horse's head was probably fashioned out of papier mâché and was fixed to a stick. Here are the words of the actual play.

By your leave gentlemen all
Your pardon I do crave,
Excusing me for being so bold
To see what sport we'll have.

There's more in the company now,
They're following on behind,
They've sent us on before,
Admission for to find.

These lads they are but young,
Ne'er acted here before,
They'll do the best they can
And the best can do no more.

The horse is now brought in for the first time.

Co-oop Co-oop Co-oop.

This is my poor owd 'oss
That's carried me many a mile,
Over hedges, over ditches, over high barred gates and stiles,
But now he's growing owder.
And his nature doth decay,
He's forced to snap the shortest grass
That grows upon the 'ighway,
Poor owd 'oss.

Now when this 'oss was young sir,
And in his youth and prime,
His master rode upon him
And thought him something fine.
His pretty little shoulders,
They were so plump and round,
But now they're decayed and rotten,
I'm afraid he is not sound.
Poor owd 'oss.

His feed was once the best of corn and hay,
That ever grew in cornfields, or in a meadow lay.
He's eaten all my hay sir, he's spoil-ed all my straw,
He's neither fit to ride upon
Nor in the team to draw.
Poor owd 'oss.

His hide unto a tanner
I will so freely give,
His body to the hounds sir,
I'd rather 'im die than live,
Then hang him, whip him, stick him,
A hunting we will go,
He's neither fit to ride upon,
He is no use at all.
Poor owd 'oss.

The blacksmith is now called for, and he had to make attempts
to shoe the horse. Consequently a lot of rough play then took
place among all the members of the cast saying as they did
so:—

Now for us to shoe this 'oss, sir,
It is no use at all sir,
He would soon 'a worried the Blacksmith
and his box o' nails an all.
Poor owd 'oss.

After the fun was over drinks were called for the players and a
question put to the horse: "Could the 'oss manage a drink?"
Needless to say he could. The horse's head was, however, not
removed while he took his drink. The jaws were so arranged
that a mug or tankard could be placed inside them so that the
oss got his refreshments—to the amusement of all the spec-
tators.

*　　*　　*

There were also two games which were very much Nottinghamshire's own. One was the Eakring Ball Game, and another
was a children's game which is now never heard in the area.
The Eakring Ball Game came from the annual festival known as
the Eakring Ball Play and was formerly played each Easter
Tuesday. Old historians tell us that in ancient days this was a
great meeting for the men to have a trial at their skill at foot-
ball. The men of Eakring were even known to break the sabbath
by kicking the ball to and from church on a Sunday. The game
did not have the rules that it does now, and Mr. Briscoe, writing
in 1786, tells us that it was not long before the kicking of balls
became the kicking of shins. This kicking of shins was another
game for which this area was famous, and was pursued in place
of the wrestling which became popular in most other counties
in England.

The children's game went like this:— The children divided
into two parties, the boys and the girls. The girls all sat in a
row on what was supposed to be green grass. One of their
number was selected to play the part of the mother, and she sat
in the middle. The boys stood in a row in front of the girls with
their hands joined. When all was ready the boys began by walking or skipping four paces forward with their hands joined, and
then four paces back, saying these words:—

Stepping on the green grass,
Thus and Thus and Thus (with suitable actions),
Please will you let your daughters
Come out to play with us?

To this request the mother replied, "No". The boys, keeping up
their rhythmical movement, replied:

We will give you pots and pans
And we will give you brass,
We will give you anything,
All for a pretty lass!

71

To this the mother again said "No", and the boys continued:

We will give you gold and silver,
We will give you pearl,
We will give you anything,
All for a pretty girl!

The mother could not now refuse, so her answer was "Yes". One boy was now allowed to choose his girl, then all joined hands and galloped round in a circle singing:

She shall gallop and she shall trot,
She shall carry the mustard pot,
All around the chimney pot,
With a Hi! Ho! Hum!

When they had danced enough they started again until all the girls and boys had gone through the game. This game was still being played a century ago.